the desire to love myself

By Robyn Michelle

Copyright © 2024 by Robyn Michelle

All rights reserved. This book is protected by the copyright laws of the United States of America. No part of this publication may be reproduced, stored in a retrieval system, or transmitted in any form or by any means, electronic or mechanical, including photocopying, recording, scanning, or otherwise, except as permitted under Section 107 or 108 of the 1967 United States Copyright Act, without the prior written permission of the author. Requests to the author for permission to use should be addressed to RobynMichelle.life@gmail.com.

Mention of specific companies, organizations, or authorities in this book does not imply endorsement by the author or publisher, nor does mention of specific companies, organizations, or authorities imply that they endorse this book, its author, or the publisher. All trademarks are the property of their respective companies. Internet addresses and telephone numbers in this book were accurate when it went to press.

Limit of Liability/Disclaimer of Warranty: While the author has used her best efforts in preparing this book, she makes no representations or warranties concerning the accuracy or completeness of the contents of this book and specifically disclaims any implied warranties of merchantability or fitness for a particular purpose. The advice and strategies contained herein may not be suitable for your situation. Most people who buy any "how to" information get little to no results, especially when they aren't willing to consistently follow the suggested strategies and work hard. All personal growth and business success incur risks and require persistence and action. If the reader is not willing to accept this, please do not purchase this book.

Library of Congress Control Number: 2024925187
Published in Wilmington, NC
Publication Cataloging-in-Publication Data
Paperback ISBN: 979-8-9920625-0-2
eBook ISBN: 979-8-9920625-1-9

Printed in the United States of America

Publishing Services provided by Rebel Queen
https://rebelqueen.co/
Social media: @rebelqueenbooks

This book is dedicated to those who laugh with me until we're crying and cry with me until we're laughing.

Resiliency

Resiliency,
Resilient me.

Life is a series of ups and downs,
A constant flow,
It ebbs and flows.

Challenges, pitfalls, and heartaches abound,
They're all around,
So what do we do?

We move the rocks,
walk the fiery coals,
climb the mountains.

We overcome, we learn as we go, we grow,
We believe, we achieve, and we celebrate

Resiliency,
Resilient me.

introduction

Have you ever really spent time dreaming about the future you want for yourself? Truly take the time to allow yourself to see what it looks and feels like to live the life of your dreams. Have you truly envisioned every detail of it? Take a few moments to do that right now and take your time. Close your eyes, breathe in, and bring into focus where you see yourself five years from now, ten years from now. Do you see in vivid detail every moment of that future? How does it feel to have that perfect family, those close friends, that specific career, that long-awaited trip across the sea that you've always desired for yourself? Allow your imagination to help you fully embrace those moments, the laughter, and the memories that will be made. Visualize the big picture, then narrow in on some of the details. What do you see? Take a deep breath. Imagine what you smell. Quietly imagine what sounds you hear in the background. Allow your mind's eye to take over and see where it leads you.

Now that you have finished visualizing the life you dream of, remember how it made you feel. Did it make you feel happy, powerful, capable, successful? I hope it did. I hope the dream of your future brings you peace and joy.

My secret to you is this: you can live the life you dream of; it's not unobtainable or out of reach. No dream is too big. Dreams are your destiny and part of what makes you who you are—they are uniquely designed by you and meant specifically for you. No matter what your life looks like currently, you can begin making changes. Start taking steps towards the life you envision one day at a time, and you will achieve your goals and enjoy living the future you just imagined.

Making your dreams a reality may not happen quickly or be easy, but the key is to consistently focus your energy toward where you want to be. Find your goal and don't let anything discourage or prevent you from reaching the target. There are hundreds of stories of people who overcame obstacles to make their dreams come true. One great example is the rags-to-riches story of J.K. Rowling. As she explains in her book *Very Good Lives: The Fringe Benefits of Failure and the Importance of Imagination*, she was "…as poor as it is possible to be in modern Britain, without being homeless." Rowling bravely left her abusive husband with her young daughter and started her life over with a suitcase containing the first three chapters of Harry Potter. Rowling was barely getting by and contemplating suicide before she sought professional help and set her sights on completing her manuscript, which she did mostly in coffee shops around Edinburgh while her daughter slept. After *many* rejections, her hard work was accepted by a then-small publishing house in London. The rest of Rowling's story reads like a fairytale, as she went from near-homelessness to a billionaire in a very short ten years.

You can be one of those people who will one day tell others of your story. Providing insight into how you overcame obstacles, grew through challenges, resiliently stayed the course, and achieved your dreams. You will look back and celebrate your achievements.

Regardless of where your starting line is, fulfilling your dreams is possible. You could be in the pits of despair, uncertain how to make it through each day, or perhaps you are stuck going through the motions expected of you. No matter where you are and what the reason is, you can stop, change direction and rechart your path toward turning your dreams into reality.

I am your loyal advocate, your faithful encourager, and your enthusiastic supporter. I hope to give you enough motivation to send you in the direction of your dreams. I want to also reassure you that no matter what you may be facing, you're not alone. There is strength in numbers. Let's stop hiding our struggles and start talking about what we're going through so we can lift each other up and accomplish more together.

We are now embarking on a journey through life's toughest battles—experiencing hardships, believing life is more than the difficulties we face, overcoming adversity, and moving forward toward the future we desire and deserve. I encourage you to push yourself to work hard, overcome, and achieve your goals so you can live your best life

Ready? Okay, take one more deep breath, and let's begin this journey together.

"you can live the life you dream of"

a desert island

When watching a movie like *Cast Away* or television series such as *Naked and Afraid*, I often think to myself, "Could I survive if I were stranded on a desert island?" Survival-type shows always get my problem-solving brain thinking. Maybe that thought or something similar has crossed your mind too. "What would I do in their place? What could I bring myself to kill, or what would I eat to survive? If it were to rain, what would I do?" To say I dislike being wet and cold is an understatement. I'm not a Girl Scout, and I have no survival skills or wilderness training of any kind, but I'm sure we've all mentally thought through various scenarios while watching nature versus mankind type of television shows. I'd like to think I could build a decent shelter, but I'm certain I'd starve pretty quickly, be utterly sick from sun poisoning, and freeze to death at night. If you're taking odds on my survival, don't bother—just send help!

Thankfully, here I am—not only surviving but thriving! Far from a desert island, my cute little Coastal Carolina beach town is far from everyone and everything I know. I moved five hundred miles away to be on my own for the first time in forty-five years. Knowing nothing about the area—other than it has outstanding weather for a summer-lover like me—I chose to be close to the beach and decided it was time for a change. This was an opportunity to alter my life for the better, and I didn't want it to pass me by.

So often we say to ourselves, "One day I'm going to…" But then that one day turns into another and another, and it doesn't come. It never comes. So many other things come up, one after another, that keep you from that *one day* until eventually you tuck it away, deep in your heart, and brush it off as something that just wasn't meant to be. Occasionally you'll take it out, examine it, and from time to time when stargazing, wonder what might have been, then put it back on the shelf and proceed with life as usual.

Not me, not this time. This was my time. Much like a survival show, in my new wilderness I had to learn how to navigate the basics of survival: locating resources (finding a job to have an income), finding shelter (a place to live and call home), securing provisions (finding a new grocery store—I sure hoped they had an ALDI!). Then I had to go beyond the basics and get a new health care provider, ensure I had a reliable car that was covered by AAA in case I needed assistance, and switch internet providers. Anyone who has moved knows there are many details to sort, but this was my first solo journey and I had much to learn. While I'm still not over Comcast's inability to move with me to North Carolina, at least I don't have to worry about eating any berries that might cause a slow, painful death.

You may be asking, "Why the drastic change halfway through your forties?" Or maybe you want to know why I'd be crazy enough to do it on my own. I'm happy to share the events that led me to take a huge leap of faith and pursue my dreams. I hope doing so empowers you to embrace your life, points you in the direction of your dreams, and gives you enough courage to pursue them.

Also be assured, pursuing dreams and achieving goals doesn't have to be the result of a tragic, painful-yet-wonderful story. For those such as myself, it might be, but it can be the constant pursuit of whatever sets your soul on fire. Oftentimes the road is full of distractions, difficulties that derail us, and naysayers planting seeds of doubt that keep us from trying. All of these can knock us off course, but none of them should keep us from the outcome we desire.

As I share pieces of myself and my story with you, I hope you'll be encouraged to know it's never too late to dream a new dream and find your way to a better future.

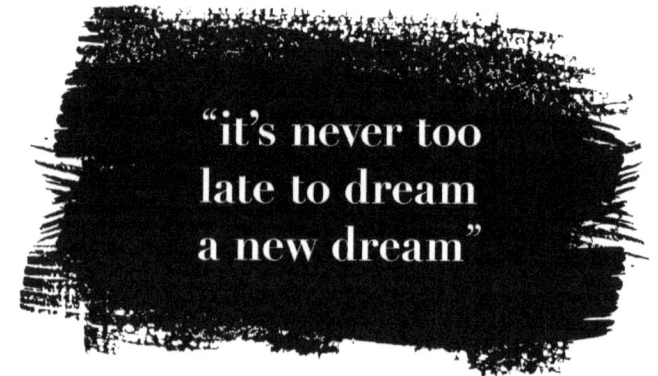

grow through what you go through

Has life ever put a stumbling block in your path that you never saw coming? At times, it's an almost invisible root and we stumble, catch ourselves, and keep on going just fine. Other times it's a giant log smashing right into our shins, bruising our legs, knocking our shoes off, and completely derailing us from the path we were happily walking. We'd be hard-pressed to find someone who can honestly say they've never faced a challenge or heartache that set them back or knocked them off course. When these moments occur, it can be a fight to find the strength to just be okay. In these moments, I challenge you to embrace the struggle.

Being knocked down provides the opportunity to get back up stronger than before. While being punched in the gut sucks a big one, it can show you how incredibly tough you are. Carry the world on your shoulders, because then you will find out just how strong you are. Let the haters and gossipers talk because you'll get to feel the satisfaction that comes when they're silenced. Embrace every challenge, letting your passion be set on fire through a heart of resilience.

You do not have to be okay with what you're going through, of course, but *use it*. Use what impacted you to empower you—to be a driving force propelling you toward what is next, toward your true calling. As you maneuver through life's obstacles, ask yourself, "What can I learn? How can I grow? How can I serve the needs of others, change my surroundings, and help my community?" As you continue moving forward and learn the answers to those questions, ask yourself, "What can I change, and what steps do I need to take so I can be where I want to be—where I am meant to be?"

Robert Frost said, "The best way out is always through," and honestly, it's the only way. As much as we want to, there is no way to avoid a situation before you and the emotions entangled with it. You must experience and endure it as best as you can while moving steadily through it. Choosing not to do so only prolongs the inevitable.

Frost's famous words were sent to me amid the most jaw-dropping, heartbreaking, soul-crushing time of my life. I will never forget them; they will forever be etched to the core of my being. I will always remember the feeling that came over me as I read them, and how deeply my heart sank. As true as they are, they were the last words I wanted to hear, as at that very moment I was struck with the realization of how difficult the road ahead would truly be. All I wanted to do was avoid what was before me, and either go back in time or skip to the good part. You see, I had just discovered my husband was having an affair. We'd only been married for five years, but I was madly in love with him and completely blindsided by this discovery.

A few weeks prior he said he was unhappy, but I thought we could work on our marriage, make some positive changes for the both of us and fix what seemed to be breaking down. Little did I know

I was engaging in what would inevitably become a losing battle. His mind and his heart had already been given to another. The most heartbreaking part was that this was my second marriage, the one that was supposed to be blessed, supposed to work out, the one I thought I deserved after surviving a sixteen-year marriage plagued by verbal and mental abuse. In my first marriage, we stayed together far too long, but did it for the kids, and because "that's what good Christians do." When it escalated to him threatening to kill me in front of our son, I finally found the strength to walk away. Did I think he would follow through with the threat? No. But that was the moment I decided our children deserved a better example of a loving relationship and I deserved peace.

It took many months for me to move forward after each marriage. I didn't want to move through it; I barely wanted to move at all. I refused to feel anything after being knocked down, and I rejected any concept of finding a blessing in the trauma. My life was shattered, and I did not have any desire to pick up and piece together whatever shards remained. But day by day, I did. Much like rainbows only come after it rains, I slowly began to see specks of color again. I started asking myself, "What do I want out of life? Who do I want to be? Where do I want to end up? What opportunities can I create for myself that I couldn't have or wouldn't have thought about before, and what steps do I need to take to make them happen?" As I began to move forward, I was determined to take control and stay in charge of my life, and you can too!

setbacks

Let's view setbacks as stepping stones. With a positive mindset, perseverance, and a plan, setbacks provide an opportunity to continually evaluate our goals and keep moving forward.

When you think about grief and going through the grieving process, compare it to going on a hike. It's not a walk in the park where the entire path is paved, you can see what's ahead of you, and you can predict what's coming. There are peaks and valleys, rocks and tree roots that trip us up, and we don't always know what's around the next turn. There will be a time when you think you're well past anger, but there will come a day or two or several along the way where unexpected waves of emotions resurface, and you are back in those emotions or feelings you had in the beginning. It can hit you out of nowhere, and leave you flabbergasted. You may find yourself thinking, "What's going on here? Where did these feelings come from? I thought I was doing so well. I thought I had moved past this." An object or event might trigger those feelings; you could hear a song, smell a candle, see something on TV, or be out and about. It could be as simple as a gentle heartstring tug, then suddenly overwhelming feelings and emotions take you by surprise. Those emotions may make you feel like you've been hit by a freight train, and that's okay. You can feel this pain and ride it out until the train is out of sight. Embrace whatever you're feeling and tell yourself this: "Not every day has to be or will be a ten-out-of-ten, dancing-in-the-kitchen kind of day." It's okay to have a two-out-of-ten kind of day. It too shall pass, and those crummy days help you appreciate the days that are nines and tens a little bit more.

When you feel like something has set you back a notch, don't endure it alone. Please feel your feelings. Always give yourself the grace to experience your true emotions because remember, the only way out of the setback is through it. Momentarily embrace how you feel, then release it. I encourage you not to stay in a place of gloom and doom for too long. When you're down and out and in a negative space, call on your tribe. Talk, cry, yell if you need to, and surround yourself with those who bring you comfort and lift you up. Some people truly want to be there for you and might be upset to learn you needed help but didn't reach out. Let them support you; lean on them.

Many times, I've simply told a friend, "I'm struggling today," and whether we talked on the phone, or they told me to come over, by the time we hung up or I headed home, we were both laughing. The weight I was carrying always felt lighter after that, and I knew I was headed in the right direction.

you are seen

For most of my life, I felt invisible. Not the type of invisible where I could get away with anything I wanted (which would've been awesome; did someone say invisibility cloak?), but where I was a wallflower fading invisibly into the background, unnoticeable. I felt mostly unmemorable, a plain Jane making very little impact on others or the world around me. On a few standout occasions, I recall someone recognizing me when running into them at the grocery store, and I was truly surprised they knew my name. I never thought I was worth remembering, so I was shocked when someone did.

In middle school and high school, I was very introverted. I had friends but wasn't popular, and only came out of my shell around those closest to me. To this day, a few teasing instances vividly stand out to me, and at the time I remember feeling embarrassed but not largely affected. At times I was mocked for my limited wardrobe, down to the shoes I wore. My stepmom and dad chose not to spend their money on things they deemed luxuries, name-brand clothes and shoes included. I wanted to look nice but ended up with a closet primarily filled with the same sweatshirt in eight different colors and a few favorite pairs of jeans. The classic all-white Reeboks my mom got me became my most prized possession, and when one pair wore out, I excitedly replaced them with a new pair of the same shoe.

This is most likely where my current clothes addiction comes from, beginning the day I received my first paycheck from my first job. Every bit of that $5.25 per hour went to New York and Company. To this day

I buy more clothes even though I still wear the same eight favorite items every day. I mean, who doesn't need twenty-eight different black T-shirts? It's familiar and comfortable and it's what I had growing up. I try time and time again to experiment with bold colors and patterns but always resort to the basic color palette that feels safe. Perhaps the teasing affected me more than I realized, because it seemed to be an under-the-radar memory, only to reappear thirty years later. But such is life and our complicated psyche.

After high school, I married quickly. The majority of my first marriage was spent being told I only had friends because my husband had friends. He would argue that no one liked me. They liked him, and therefore me by default. Though I knew it wasn't true, and have accepted it isn't true, words—especially those repeated by someone you choose to pour love into—make an impact. The assortment of harsh words spoken for years was incredibly damaging to a fragile soul already struggling with self-esteem and confidence. No matter how many friends I made, the challenges I overcame, or the successes I had, those words were constantly reiterated, so no matter how happy I was with life, or how content I felt with my little place in the world, I still felt invisible, unmemorable, and insignificant.

Over time, as I gained more independence and built up my confidence, I became less surprised when people remembered my face or my name and would approach me. I started feeling less uncomfortable when complimented and began to open up more. From time to time, that timid girl who still felt unsure about herself would resurface, until one day someone said three simple words that resonated deeply and stayed with me: "You are seen."

Take a moment to pause, ingest these words and the depth of their meaning, and know it's true—you are seen. No matter what anyone else's advice or opinions are, what you've been through, what you're currently going through, or what the voice in your head tells you—*you are seen*.

What does it mean to be seen? It means you're not alone; you're beautifully and masterfully created, you have the power to do amazing things, you matter, and you are inherently valuable.

Please believe this.

self-care

From the age of eighteen, most of my jobs have been under the umbrella of human services. Self-care has been a common term in this field for decades, due to how mentally and physically draining it is to work with others. The desire to help people but not always being able to, at times being taken for granted, and helping others to the point of exhaustion has a multitude of side effects. If we don't prioritize rest and recuperation, and allow it to go unchecked, it leads to burnout, but many of us wouldn't have it any other way, as we have an insane desire to solve the world's problems, one individual at a time.

The importance of self-care has caught on much more widely in recent years as evidenced by the first question I was asked in my last interview: "What do you do for fun when you get off work to decompress?" I am thankful for the widespread realization of its importance because you can't pour from an empty bucket. You're unable to save someone else if you are drowning. It is widely known whether you've heard a flight attendant's safety demonstration or not, when the plane is going down, you're instructed to first put your oxygen mask on before assisting others—you can't help the person sitting next to you if you can't breathe. These are things most of us know but tend to forsake in our desire to help.

Sometimes, it's not easy to practice self-care, and self-care doesn't look the same for everyone. Depending on the season of life you're in, and what's been thrown your way, carving out time for yourself to prioritize your needs may come easy or it may be a challenge. It can mean surrounding yourself with others, or it may mean finding solitude, being active, or being still. Whatever the case may be, you'll know what you need when you need it. You must listen to what your mind and your body are telling you and comply with your body's needs. It is important to intentionally take care of yourself, mentally and physically. Being strong doesn't mean pushing through and saying, "I'm fine," when you really aren't, it means taking care of your most valuable asset—*you*.

When life is good, self-care for me involves riding my bike, going to the beach, hanging with friends, going to the movies, or taking a long walk while listening to music. After my husband left, self-care looked vastly different. A short walk around the block, journaling, and binge-watching "Grace and Frankie" was all I could bring myself to do—it was all I had the energy and mental capacity for, and that's okay.

There is a mountain of things that get in the way when it comes to self-care. Being a new parent, starting a business, moving to a new house or a new city, or being surrounded by those who constantly take without appreciation or reciprocation—the list is endless. However, in these situations, it is even more vital to take a moment to think about your needs and act accordingly. This is not a selfish action on your part. This is a necessary step to begin your self-care process and form better habits that benefit you and those around you.

Think about some of the things you enjoy and write a list of those hobbies or activities. Are you someone who enjoys sun, sand, and waves, or more of a mountain person? Would you rather participate in indoor or outdoor activities? Do you prefer the peace and solitude of being alone, or being surrounded by people in an energetic environment? Whatever it is that brings peace, passion, and joy into your life, be intentional about setting aside time to fill your bucket with those activities.

Make a list now of the things that bring you peace and joy and consider how to intentionally incorporate them into your routine.

1.

2.

3.

4.

5.

attitude of gratitude

That which has happened or may be happening now is not happening to you but happening for you. Stay with me a minute, as I know there are things in life that are so tragic and unfair. Whatever it is, you have the power to take those events or circumstances and turn them into good, to take what's impacted you and use it to empower you. Depending on your current situation, or where you are in life's journey, that may not be what you want to hear or it may be difficult to process. After learning about my second husband's affair or while enduring the verbal and mental abuse of my first marriage, I was not at all receptive to hearing that what I was experiencing was "to my benefit." I wasn't even open to hearing I was going to be okay.

As time goes on, we begin to heal, our hearts soften, our minds open, the inner strength we possess is eventually revealed and we're finally able to start changing our mindset. We can go from feeling stuck, isolated or helpless to feeling empowered, strengthened, capable and ready to move forward and take on the world. Two time Triathlon World Champion Siri Lindley said in a podcast interview "everything great in my life has come out of such struggle." When we start to see things from this point of view and are grateful for each day, we recognize how our circumstances mold us into the individuals we're meant to become. We realize the things that we once viewed as negative, didn't happen to us, but happened to stretch and grow us in new ways so we can become better versions of ourselves.

The smallest, simplest thing can soften our hearts and open our minds: looking out the window one day and seeing the first sign of spring, spotting a full moon on a clear, starry night, or receiving an out-of-the-blue text from a friend you haven't heard from in a while. It may not be a knock over the head, but more of a gentle whisper or a quick wink to your soul—it's exactly what you need, in the exact moment you need it. Oftentimes, the simplest things lead to greater understanding and clarity for our future.

During an annual girls' weekend trip to the mountains after learning of my husband's affair I had my moment of clarity. I can't share too much, because "What happens at Bitter Goose Lodge, stays at Bitter Goose Lodge," but this particular trip was very different than the previous trips I had taken with my friends. Rather than engaging in the typical girls' weekend-away shenanigans, I spent this weekend reading, journaling, sitting in quiet reflection by the fire, talking quietly with my friends, and I finally realized there is freedom found in forgiveness.

Once I was able to forgive, peace came over me. I don't know who said it first, or who said it better, Rick Warren, Tony Robbins, or Ted Lasso, but "Forgiveness is a gift you give to yourself." It was then I was finally able to adopt an attitude of gratitude. I started asking myself, "What can I find to be thankful for? What are some things I can learn from this situation? How can I use this to be a better version of myself and how can I use this to propel myself into the direction of my true destiny?"

Ask yourself those questions and spend some time thinking about your answers. If you can, write down your answers to these questions; it can be quite revealing. Journaling allows for reflection through documentation and opens the door to self-discovery. You may even surprise yourself with the insight you gain. Journal where you are, the things you're working to overcome, where you hope to be, and how you plan to get there. Once you're in a better place you can look back and see where you've succeeded, which areas may still need some work, and have insight and clarity for moving forward. It's an ongoing process.

Life-changing things begin to happen when you start discovering answers to these questions. Changes typically start within yourself and then in the world around you. You may become more self-aware and more self-confident. You may be able to more easily recognize your strengths and not allow others to devalue them. You may begin to desire more from life and actively pursue your heart's desires. Before you know it, you'll be on a new path—the path meant for you.

Make a list of ten things you're grateful for. Not long ago I tried this exercise myself, got to about seven, and stopped because I didn't know what else to put down. I had listed my family, friends, my job, things I possessed, and even a recent trip I was able to take. It was all the typical things people think of when someone asks, "What are you thankful for?", and I thought, "That's it," but the list required ten, so I had some thinking to do. I pushed on, and as I added more items to the list, the content of my list changed from *things I have* to *the person I am*. Looking back at how far I've come, the healing I've done, and how comfortable I am with myself, I am so thankful. I also discovered as I looked inward rather than outward, the things I'm grateful for poured out of me much more readily. I made my list of ten and was able to keep going.

Ten Things to Be Grateful For:

1.

2.

3.

4.

5.

6.

7.

8.

9.

10.

There are positive outcomes that stem from gratitude writing, whether you write daily or weekly. I encourage you to regularly write and reflect, and I'd love to hear the impact it has on your life—when you're ready to share.

time is fleeting

I recently watched a Facebook reel showing a side-by-side comparison of your current self and your younger self using an AI filter. At the discovery of what AI is capable of, my mind is continually blown. The song "Forever Young" played, and I teared up. I was tempted to download the app and try it for myself; I still might. But as I watched the faces of those in the reel, it felt like their expressions easily gave away the thoughts going through their minds, and it was the same thing going through mine: "Where has the time gone? Did I do everything I intended with the time that I had? Did I take advantage of every opportunity? Do those close to me know how much they mean to me? Is it too late to conquer some of those mountains?" The length of time we have left lessens the more we age, and these consequent questions inevitably arise when that realization hits us in full force.

Time is fleeting. As a child, it seems we have nothing but time, summer is endless, and adulthood is beyond our grasp. Looking back as an adult, it's a different story—everything has gone by in the blink of an eye. As my kids are now grown, at times I reflect and spend time thinking about some of my favorite memories. I remember at times thinking how slowly time was passing and how much time I had with them before they turned eighteen and would be off on their own. Sometimes, I'd think, "It's going to take forever for them to grow up!" Other times I'd think, "I hope they always stay this little." Now they're grown and I often say, "They keep getting older, but I don't know how, because I haven't gotten any older at all!" That's not true, of course. I may still feel vibrant and keep active, but I am getting older, and there's less sand in life's hourglass than there once was.

Something I feel to be true about the passage of time is that it's never too late to dream a new dream, set a new goal, or start over if you must. In your lifetime you may have to begin again many times. At all times, no matter how much sand is left in life's hourglass, it is vital to have a sense of purpose and something to live for.

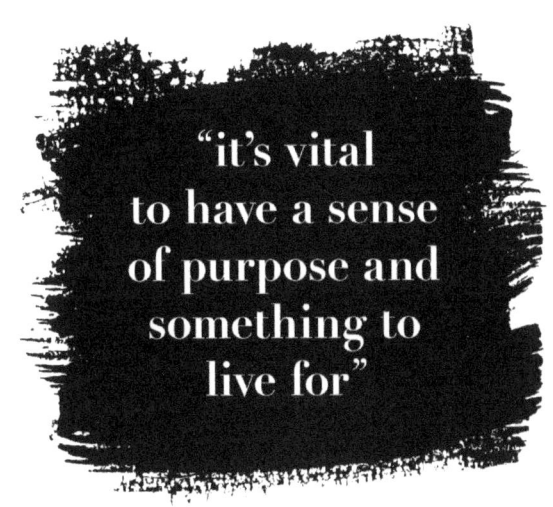

dare to disappoint

As we move forward together in the pursuit of finding what sets your soul on fire, there will be opposition. I don't believe you're reading this while wearing rose-colored glasses, and under the false impression that this road will be an easy one. We all know there will be twists, turns, dips, peaks, and sometimes fiery coals to cross on the path before us. There will be trials of many kinds to test your determination, cultivate your problem-solving abilities, and develop your character into becoming the person you need to be to achieve your goals. All these trials or challenges serve a purpose and provide lessons along the way.

It may come as a surprise when people—intentionally or unintentionally—throw stumbling blocks in your path. Whether it be naysayers or doubters, people are people. It's going to happen at some point and might even be those you'd least expect—your friends or loved ones. There may be those who try and tell you what you're doing is wrong or ridiculous. "What you're aiming to do cannot be done, your dream is too big." "What you're trying to do can be done, but you can't do it. That's for someone else." "Your idea isn't a good one." "That's a great idea, but it's not the right time to execute it."

Do it anyway! If you passionately believe it is the right course of action, you do not need anyone's approval or acceptance.

Oh, that can be difficult to get over because we so desperately seek acceptance in this world. Not this time, my friend, not this time. You're not following your heart for anyone else's satisfaction but your own. Take what they say with a grain of salt, stay resolved, and stay the course you have set for yourself.

As you do your thing, those who doubt you may show their disapproval. They may be disappointed in the decisions you make and the amount of time you dedicate to achieving your goals. They may even say that the time you've redistributed is taking away from other things in your life, such as time with them or priorities they deem more important for you. If you're keeping things in balance and harmony with your new flow of self-care, and goal-oriented lifestyle, you can block out their negativity. Dare to disappoint, because here's the thing: you don't know, nor can you control other people's reaction to your actions. Their reactions are outside of your circle of control. Focus on yourself, your goals, and the steps you're taking to better your life. If they're disappointed by that, it may be time to reevaluate their role in your life.

All hope is not lost when facing the disappointment brought on by others. Consider this, the source of their disappointment may be personal to them and have nothing to do with you. Perhaps it stems from dissatisfaction in their own lives, jealousy, or that the reality they envisioned for themselves is very different from the one that's unfolding. There could be any number of reasons they're in a negative space about your positive changes. So boldly and confidently proceed, and hope in time that their disappointment will quickly turn into admiration as they watch you prevail.

Alternatively, there is good news: you'll also come across those who show up just to cheer you on. They say, "Haters gonna hate," and they're right, but there are also people rooting for your success in more ways than you'll ever know.

connection

Human connection is one of the beautiful things that make life worth living. We're surrounded by people every day; they are and always will be part of our lives. Some are in your life from birth to death, and some are just passing through momentarily. Some are family, and some are friends you choose to make family. Others you may expect to be part of your life for the long haul, but it doesn't always work out that way. Some pop in and out, but always happen to be there when you need them the most. One thing I believe is each of these people adds value and meaning to our lives. Each of these people matter.

Every day we're moving in different directions with various things fighting for our attention. Sometimes, people come in like a hurricane and end up being the breath of fresh air you didn't know you needed. There is value to every relationship, and each interaction is a precious moment to store in your treasure box. All we can do is be thankful for the role each person played in our lives, the contributions they made, and rest in the hope that we have a spot in their treasure box as well.

I am incredibly blessed to have a variety of friendships. There are friends I consider family—we have a close bond that nothing can shake. A few of them I talk to regularly and do activities with often. Some friends I talk to occasionally due to life, distance, and priorities coming between us, making our relationships harder to maintain. Others I may not have talked to for quite some time, sometimes years, but when we do talk, we pick up right where we left off, as if nothing amiss is between us. They're all equally important to me and loved dearly.

I've found that we always seem to have exactly who we need, exactly when we need them. One friend, whom I rarely kept in touch with for over twenty years, helped me move my things hundreds of miles without hesitation or asking any questions. She was a great friend for a long time, then life happened, as it does. We became busier and went in separate directions for a while. We stayed in touch, primarily through liking each other's social media posts, and saw each other at the occasional baby shower or graduation party. Neither of us ever felt bad about drifting apart because we both understand it happens. But our love, respect, and close bond—the kind that says, "I'm always here for you," stayed intact, and in time of great need, so she was indeed.

Dear reader, no matter where you are or what you're going through, never discount friends you've lost contact with or don't feel as close to. It's okay to feel sadness if the composition of your friendships has changed over the years, as it can happen. Change brings a natural course of growth and separation. I have a dear friend whom I grew much closer to after moving five hundred miles away than the two of us ever felt when she lived just ten minutes down the road. Another friend I lost touch with now lives in the town where I currently reside, and despite the years that passed, it's as if nothing has changed between us. We picked up right where we left off.

It's normal and natural as time goes on, our lives evolve and we become involved with our careers, our growing families, and our increasingly busy lives that our friendship dynamics change. Wise friends understand this but still choose to be there when they're most needed. However, the key to having those friends there is to ask and communicate. Truthfully share with them what is taking place in your life, and don't be afraid to open up. Walking around with a smile to hide pain, suffering, or struggles isn't going to help you in the long run, nor will it help others gauge how you're really doing. This could lead them to assume you're fine when you're not. Those who truly care about you would be upset or saddened to know you needed assistance, but never gave them the opportunity to be by your side. You're selling their help short, depriving them of the opportunity to grow with you by coming alongside you to offer help and support.

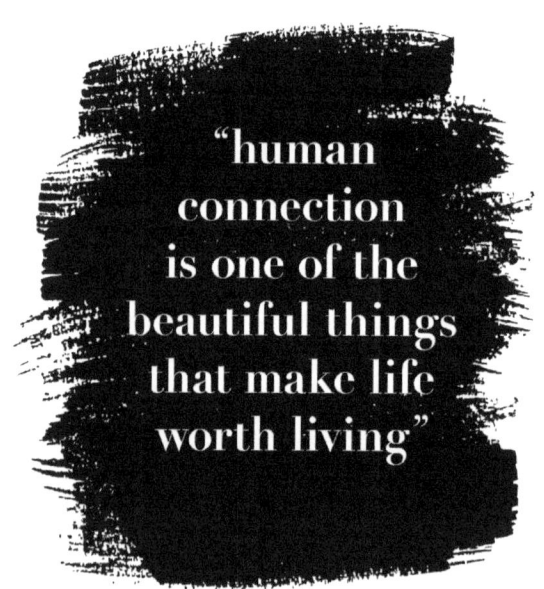

"human connection is one of the beautiful things that make life worth living"

all alone

Perhaps you're asking, "What if I have no friends at all? What if I'm truly one hundred percent all alone, on my own?" I can assure you I've had those same thoughts and feelings. One of the first things I did after moving south was to join several community Facebook groups. There seems to be something for everyone and everything! I determined it would be a great way to learn about the town, events happening nearby, where things are located, and maybe make a few new friends. I also figured at the at the very least joining a few community Facebook pages would be extremely entertaining. IYKYK (If you know, you know)! I found myself surprised by how many posts I saw from people looking for friendship, asking where to meet others with similar interests, sharing real struggles about feeling isolated, and publicly expressing true vulnerability.

The town I moved to is a salad bowl of diversity, and people everywhere are moving at lightning speed due to financial reasons, careers, proximity to beautiful beaches, or simply a desire for change—leaving familiarity, life-long friends, and family behind. Making new friends isn't easy for everyone and can be especially challenging for young families who feel isolated by their family obligations. As we age it can become more challenging to make just one new friend. It's not like Jenny across the street is going to knock on your door and ask you to come outside and play while the moving van is still unloading. Because of how political and harmful the world has become, everyone is overly cautious, suspicious, and careful nowadays. No one dares to bring you cookies or a casserole when you're new to the neighborhood. It's rare to even get an introduction. Everyone keeps to themselves to avoid offending someone, even if it's accidental.

But through Facebook, I discovered there were moms stuck at home with no adult interaction, twenty-somethings looking for friends with similar interests, and fifty-somethings not knowing where to meet people in a town seemingly overrun with twenty-somethings. So, they all turned to social media to try and find connections, and you know what? Good for them for using their resources and reaching out. You can't get answers to questions you don't ask. You've heard the saying, "The only dumb question is the one not asked?" Not only did the online community rally behind those bold enough to ask by offering suggestions on where to meet people, what to do, where to go, and even offer to meet up at the park, but they were also empathetic, understanding, and encouraging. Not something you always see on social media, but definitely refreshing. Disclaimer: when utilizing online resources, always exercise caution when connecting with anyone—meet in public, share your location with someone you trust, have an exit strategy, and be cautious about giving away too much personal information.

I like to encourage finding friends through mutual interests. Consider what you enjoy, what hobbies you like, or what goals you are working towards. As you dive into these areas of interest and find outlets that support your personal growth, you're likely to meet like-minded people with similar interests and a shared life path.

If you find yourself feeling isolated or lacking connection, this is the time to be brave, be bold, speak up, and put yourself out there. Once you have, don't stop; keep doing it until you no longer feel adrift or alone at sea. We aren't meant to do life alone. Eventually, you'll find the connections or relationships you're looking for, and realize your people were out there waiting to meet you too.

friends gone by

I believe every person admitted into your life has been allowed in for a reason. Consider wholeheartedly embracing this: some people come into your life for a short time, but their impact is no less valuable or significant than those you've spent years getting to know and love. Whether it be for a few moments, or a few months, for days, or years, each person's presence has a purpose in your life.

Sometimes, the impact someone has on our lives can be revealed instantly. There may be a feeling we receive from their presence; they have "good vibes." Perhaps we feel a sense of peace and calmness by being around them, almost like they center our emotions. Maybe this revelation happens when they say something that rings true for us and it hits deeply becoming something we ponder, aren't able to let go of, which then sets off a chain reaction of events, causing us to act and sending us in a new, unexpected direction. Can you think of anyone who has had this type of impact in your life?

Other times we may not understand a person's impact until long after they're gone from our lives, like the high school teacher we took for granted, who tried to give us sage advice. We didn't recognize or appreciate it at the time, and then we graduate and make our way into the world, we think we're ready for anything. We leave them behind, forgetting their impact until the world ushers us into harsh realities, and we're reminded of their investment of time, kindness, and care—and all the things we wish we'd paid more attention to.

At times it's age and sometimes it's experience, but as life goes on there are moments when we look back on these relationships and appreciate their impact and value in a new way. We're able to retrospectively analyze these connections and ask, "Was that a positive relationship, or is it a blessing that they're no longer part of my life?" Good or bad, we're meant to learn something from each one—nothing is coincidental, it all serves a bigger purpose. We can take the positive experiences and hold them in our hearts, take negative experiences and learn from them, and with greater wisdom from both, move forward accordingly.

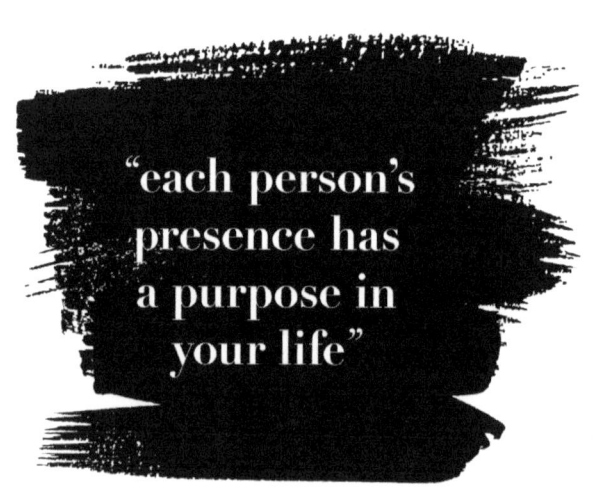

"each person's presence has a purpose in your life"

hurtful people

Whether it's accidental or intentional, none of us expect to be hurt by those we care about, but it happens because people are imperfect. I know I've both been hurt and have hurt others, but no matter who, when, or what the circumstance, it always seems to come as a surprise to one or both parties involved. People closest to us are often the last ones we suspect of bringing any sort of pain into our lives, but inevitably they're often the ones capable of inflicting the most pain, because of how much of ourselves we pour into those relationships. The wounds we suffer from our closest allies often produce the deepest cuts. If we didn't care about them so much, their actions or words would have little impact, but there are times when those closest to us, our dear friends and loved ones, those who we thought would be our greatest champions, can be the ones leaving us with the deepest wounds and in the most shock. As it was said in Julius Caesar, "Et tu, Brutus?"

Disappointment and hurt can teach us how to stand up for ourselves, recognize and more clearly define our boundaries, and fight for what we believe to be right and true. Throughout my journey of healing after the affair, I shared my opinion, with love and compassion, about the hurt my friends or loved ones caused. This was part of my healing process and I felt I needed to do so to move forward. I chose to share my honest thoughts so they'd know how I felt and be held accountable, and maybe my honesty would help bring light to the situation and they would know; how you treat people matters. Everything they said or did truly affected me, and I needed them to know that my sole intention was to create a better way of communicating between us. What was done was done. Best case scenario, maybe it would change how they communicate with others moving forward. I believe it's important to share our feelings with grace but know they won't always be met with an open heart and an open mind. When communicating how I felt with those I cared about, I expected nothing in return. How the other person receives what you say and chooses to react is in their hands. Continue to be a gentle, kind, and gracious soul, and don't let the fear of others' reactions keep you from sharing your truth or worse, make you think your feelings are invalid or misplaced.

Going through my divorce, I shared my truth with some of those who hurt me the most: a few close friends, my husband, and the pastor who married us. Some friends made flimsy excuses, and others ignored my feelings entirely. When I gained the strength to approach my husband, my cries were met with silence. I earnestly expressed the pain that gripped me, only to feel like I was facing a brick wall alone. There was no remorse, no apology, no compassion. He was expressionless. Not one word in response. Once I had spoken my truth, I quietly left.

I conversed with my pastor via text, expressing my disappointment in not only the lack of support by the man who provided marriage counseling and joined us together but also in his total absence during this time in our lives. He was there for our union, yet absent during the dissolution of our marriage. My communication was met with deflection. He took no ownership over his absence, lack of support, or how things could have been handled differently, and no responsibility for his leadership role. There was no asking how I was doing, or if I needed continued support, no "I'm sorry *I let you down*." Instead, he said, "I'm sorry you *felt* let down," a non-apology apology.

I wasn't expecting any peace from their responses or any extended conversations. I found peace in the release of it all as I let it go, and in doing so, was able to move forward.

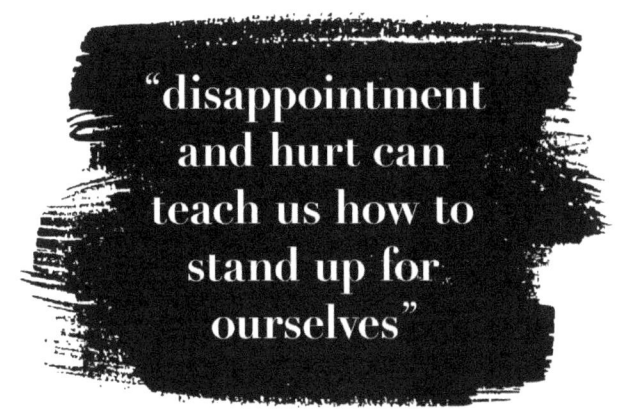

confidence is contagious

Vince Lombardi once said, "Confidence is contagious, so is [a] lack of confidence." This has been scientifically proven[1] to be one of the main reasons extremely successful entrepreneurs reach high levels of success. They aren't just confident, they're *overly* confident. They take risks where others won't. They convince people that goals aren't just obtainable, but that failure is unfathomable. A future without their inventions, machines, mechanisms, or creative solutions is presented as a world that doesn't even make sense. Their confidence is so high and so contagious that everyone buys into what they're selling and follows without a second thought.

I thank my father for instilling the importance of confidence in me. My father, whom I haven't heard from or spoken to in over twenty years, who's never met his beautiful, amazing grandchildren, who kicked me out of the house just weeks before my high school graduation because I engaged in good, old-fashioned, typical Generation X youth shenanigans. Yes, this father. I am thankful for constantly hearing,

---

1 Geoffrey James, "According to Neuroscience, Confidence Is Contagious, but Not for the Reasons You Think | Inc.Com," Inc., November 8, 2019, https://www.inc.com/geoffrey-james/if-youve-got-this-1-character-trait-youll-probably-be-successful-according-to-neuroscience.html.

"You can do anything you set your mind to" throughout my formative years. There was no shortage of confidence building as I grew up. Although for quite a long period of time my confidence dwindled, those seeds of confidence were planted throughout my adolescent years that I was able to water and thus began to grow once I regained my independence and surrounded myself with the right people.

Thanking someone who has severed relations may seem bizarre, but this is another relationship I've healed from, and hold no animosity toward. It's another reminder that we can find something to be thankful for within the role each person played in our lives and the contributions they made, even if they're no longer an active part of our lives.

As you continue to purposely take steps towards personal growth, I want you to adopt this same principle because I really do believe you can do anything you set your mind to. Do you have someone telling you this same truth? If so, that's great! If not, look in the mirror and tell yourself, "I can do this." Listen to those words and make them your new mantra. Next, say the thing you have your heart set on accomplishing. Write it on a Post-it and put it on your mirror so it's the first thing you see every morning. "I can do this. I can do anything I set my mind to. I can (insert the goal you want to achieve)!"

We receive back what we put out into this world, tenfold—gratitude and confidence included. Put your energy toward the things you want and speak confidently over them as if *they're already yours*. Keep your head held high and a firm resolve—you're going to conquer the world and crush all your goals. *You've got this*—and it's only a matter of time!

positive self-talk

Growing up, my dad was really into reading books in the genre of motivational/self-help, positive thinking, and leadership. After he would devour these books, he regularly passed on the knowledge he gained from his reading to the rest of the family. At one time, our family's bookshelves were adorned with my mother-in-law's collection of Danielle Steele on one side and books written by Dale Carnegie, Norman Vincent Peale, and similar authors on the other. He loved to constantly remind us how special we were and that we could do anything we set our minds to. He also loved to constantly remind us of the power of positive thinking. I encourage you to adopt similar habits and speak to or about yourself positively.

As I mentioned previously, there was no shortage of confidence building growing up in my childhood home. I believe that encouragement and constant positivity helped to shape my optimistic outlook, despite the negativity that encompassed my first marriage. I believe that constructive thinking not only helped shape my outlook, but, in some ways, provided a protective barrier that I was unaware even existed during a time it was most needed. Because of this, I encourage you to speak to and about yourself positively and do this often. Not only is it important to be kind to yourself and give yourself grace, but it's also important to have the courage to believe others when they do the same—because *you are worthy*.

What does your inner dialogue tell you daily? Does it inspire you to believe in yourself and your abilities? Does it build your confidence and encourage you to reach your full potential? Most importantly, are you able to recognize if your thoughts are positive or self-critical? Ask yourself, "Would I say these things to my best friend?" "Would I say these things to my child?" or "How would I feel if someone else talked to me like this?" If your thoughts toward yourself are not something you would say to encourage another or find encouraging from someone else, then take a moment, pause, and turn any negatives into positives one thought at a time.

As the saying goes, "You are the company you keep." The same can be said of your thoughts: "You are the thoughts you think." Phrases I often heard during my formative years include, "You can do anything you set your mind to," "Dream big," and "Can't isn't a word." My dad never allowed the word "can't" in our home. Any time I said it, he would make me repeat the sentence, reframe it, and replace "can't" with "can." Very annoying to a fourteen-year-old, but it's an impactful practice, and so very true. Saying "I can't" is also a difficult habit to break once stuck in that mindset. I know this due to how many times I was stopped in my tracks to repeat and reframe my sentences. "I can't," is essentially equivalent to: "I won't," "Why bother?" or "Don't even try, because you'll fail." When you say, "I can," you give yourself the permission and motivation to take steps forward, to try, and to give it a go and see what happens. Maybe you'll make a mistake or two before being successful, but each time you can learn, tell yourself "I can do this," and try again. Eventually, you'll succeed because you keep telling yourself you can until there's no room for doubt. Saying "can't" will hold you back. Saying "can" will propel you forward. I learned how to do a lot of things using the word "can" that I may not have otherwise invested time in learning.

imposter syndrome

Occasionally, I astonish myself with the things I say in meetings or on the phone while at work when talking to my leaders, clients, or community partners—I sound so knowledgeable and professional. It sometimes feels like I'm looking at myself from the outside; experiencing an out-of-body experience, and I am watching myself and asking, "Who even *is* that person? She seems to really know what she's talking about!"

On the outside, I feel unworthy, incapable, and like someone far more qualified should be filling these shoes. This overwhelming feeling surfaces from time to time and has over the course of my entire life sporadically no matter where I have worked, what project I've worked on, or how knowledgeable I may be.

Impostor syndrome rears its ugly head and I ask myself, "Who am I?" "Who do I think I am?" In these moments it's critical to quickly remind ourselves who we are, as one tiny bit of negative self-talk can send you spiraling down a rabbit hole, paralyzed.

Intrusive thoughts may cross your mind, and if they do, it's important to intentionally turn these thoughts around; give yourself a pep talk and flood your mind with positive affirmations. Remind yourself who you are. Tell yourself, "I am good enough, I am smart enough, I am bold enough, I am strong enough, and I can do this. I am worthy." Then, find the courage to be proud of yourself, because you could've allowed those negative thoughts to incapacitate you—but you didn't.

I have six positive affirmations written on sticky notes stuck to the mirror in my bathroom. I begin each day by brushing my teeth, washing my face, and reading each one aloud. It's a great way to jump-start the day and become mentally strong for what the day may bring.

If you are interested in giving it a try, get some sticky notes for your bathroom mirror in your favorite color and a marker. I've listed some affirmations to get you started or perhaps you've thought of some of your own.

I matter

I have value

I believe in my abilities

I trust my intuition

I accept myself fully and unconditionally

I have everything I need for success

a growth mindset

I did things a little unconventionally when carrying out my "success sequence." in life. I graduated high school, fell in love, started a family, and then decided I wanted to go to college and continue my education. When I graduated high school, I didn't know what I wanted out of life or what I wanted my future to look like. My friends and those I graduated high school with all seemed to have their paths laid out before them, but I needed a gap year—time to figure out what I was truly passionate about and how to get from where I was to where I wanted to be. It took a while to figure it out, but when I did, I was adamantly ready.

My husband opposed my desire to further my education. I recall asking on various occasions before starting a family his thoughts on my attending school, taking classes, and furthering my education as I began to crave a more specific future and the answer was always the same. Simply no. So, I was forced to get creative when I began college. Before it became popular and common, I enrolled in online college courses. When online college classes were first introduced, many didn't believe an online degree was equivalent to a "real education." But I longed to learn and grow, and I believed in myself, so I took the plunge. I hid my classes from my husband for months, working secretly during the day while he was at work and the kids took their naps. Inevitably all things done in darkness come to light and one day my sister-in-law spilled the beans. He was pissed, we argued, but eventually he got over it when he realized I wasn't going to give up. I was proud that I stood up for myself and what I believed would be best for my future.

While in college, not only did I learn the subject matter of the classes I attended, but I also learned that gaining knowledge about something you love or are passionate about comes easily. If I could make a living out of being a student, I'd go to school for the rest of my life—it's too bad there isn't a job where you get paid to learn. People would often ask how I juggled all the things on my plate, but I never felt like I had a good answer because to me it wasn't difficult to make time for my classes or to do the assignments. I never felt like I was juggling. I graduated with my master's degree over ten years ago and I'm still learning. I may not be in school any longer and I've lost the desire to go back, but as I set new goals and work to achieve them, I immerse myself in that subject so I can accelerate my movement forward. To begin writing this book, I started going to a writing group, listening to podcasts, reading books on writing, and surrounding myself with like-minded people to educate myself from their experiences.

Embrace this mindset of growth. Every time you set a new goal or have something you are intentionally working toward immerse yourself in learning everything you can about it and keep fueling that fire. Surround yourself with like-minded people who are passionate about that same goal, read about it, research it, talk about it, and engage in activities supporting it. Not only will you learn about your passion, but you'll grow in knowledge and increase your confidence—the new force to keep propelling you forward! An additional bonus is that you'll meet and make friends with similar interests.

challenge yourself

In high school, I was the girl with a seventeen-minute mile. I know; Sadly, I didn't even try! When I did try to run on those dreaded mile-run gym class days, my thighs would become incredibly red and itchy, and I felt like I couldn't breathe. I would be so uncomfortable I thought something must be wrong with me, so I'd slow down and walk around the track, frustrating my gym teacher and making my class wait. Running was not in my blood. Fast forward almost twenty-five years. Seeking a healthy outlet post-divorce, I found it in various forms of exercise. I tried Zumba, POUND class, kickboxing, and even began running. Eventually, I ran regularly and loved it—signing up for races, texting my running buddy daily about how far we planned to go or what path we wanted to take, and spending too much on running shoes.

If you're a runner, kudos to you! I love running. If you're not a runner, I don't blame you—running sucks. I'd much rather run to the refrigerator for more queso! I have a love/hate relationship with running, and if you're a runner too, you've probably felt the same way at one point or another. I avidly ran for a while, stopped, then began running again. But when I moved to North Carolina where the humidity can hit ninety-nine percent before the sun comes up, I said, "Never again!" Now I miss it. Not really. But kind of. Maybe. See what I mean—it's a love/hate dynamic.

Through this exploration, I've come to realize we can do far more than we think if we challenge ourselves. Set a goal for yourself and set it big, because *you can achieve it!* Most often the things holding us back are ourselves, our fears, and our perception of what our limitations might be. Imagine if you had no limitations, or better yet, imagine being three years old again, not even knowing what the word "limitation" is. Now, approach life with that same fearless enthusiasm—that you can do anything and nothing can hurt you. I'm not encouraging you to jump off a cliff without a parachute, but I am encouraging you to fearlessly pursue your dreams. In doing so, you may have to do some things that take you outside of your comfort zone.

When you reach new milestones, challenge yourself to keep going—don't shy away or turn back. Remind yourself that you can do this—even if you're fearful or anxious, do it anyway.

Being taken out of our comfort zone and challenged to go beyond ourselves is how we build character. You will astonish yourself when you see what you are made of, and what you can achieve. Each broken-down barrier will build your confidence until it shines so brightly others can see it. (See how I keep coming back to confidence?) You'll learn things about yourself you didn't know before. You'll feel what it's like to excel, and it'll cause you to crave continual success.

who's your toughest critic?

If someone says, "I like your nails," "What a pretty dress," or "Your hair looks nice," what is your immediate response? If your dress has pockets, the obvious response is, "Thanks, it has pockets!" But sometimes it can be hard to receive a compliment, especially when we're struggling and feeling less than confident. Many of us tend to look in the mirror and focus on those areas we feel need improvement, while friends look at us and see only the beautiful person they know on the inside and out, and strangers might look at us and see the things that are to be admired. For some reason, we have the habit of being our own harshest critic. The things we perceive as flaws most others are entirely blind to or see as magnificent.

Every person on this planet has at least one thing they'd change about themselves if they could. For example, my tummy isn't perfectly flat, I have a discolored tooth, and I wish I could be better at putting myself out there without fearing what other people might think. Well, my tummy will never be perfectly flat—after two kids, I proudly sport the multitude of stretch marks I earned. I tried whitening my discolored tooth, but root damage from flying over bicycle handlebars in the third grade made its discoloration permanent and prominent (mostly to only myself). Others may notice my tummy or tooth and just pass them off as features that make me, me. As far as putting myself out there, I strive to do better with this daily. Through insecurity and self-consciousness, we may amplify and project our fears that someone will notice these things and unfairly judge us, but *no one notices these things as much as we do*.

I encourage you to be kinder to yourself. When someone compliments you, believe what they tell you. Smile, thank them, walk away with a renewed perspective, and pay it forward by complimenting someone else, giving them a chance to feel that same confidence. We all have room for improvement, as life is about continual growth and self-betterment. You can work on the parts of yourself you want to refine, but just know they're not flaws, they are not ugly imperfections, they're what makes you beautifully unique. I plan to work on becoming a better version of myself until the day my children exchange my freedom for a life of playing pinochle and cribbage at the senior living center—but even then, I'll want to be the best card player! Rather than negatively approaching personal growth by looking down on ourselves for what we believe are faults and imperfections, let's turn our thinking around. Remind yourself, "I am beautifully born. I accept myself completely and unconditionally and I'm continually working to be better, stronger, wiser, and the best version of me I can be."

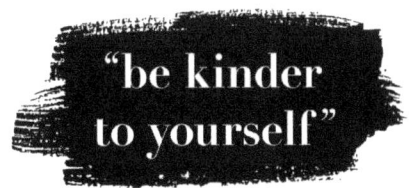

"be kinder to yourself"

broken compass

How do you keep pushing forward when you don't know which way to go? For most of my adult life, I knew exactly what I wanted to do. When I started having kids, my strongest desire was to be a stay-at-home mom. This was not an option. I was determined to do whatever was needed to stay home with them while still earning an income. I chose to create in-home childcare and was blessed to work with great families who had wonderful kids I could care for during the day. It provided the income I needed and gave me the ability to stay home. Not only was it the perfect situation, but as it turns out, I also felt like I'd found my life's calling; I loved it. As time went on, my dreams got bigger. I was still satisfied with watching kids in my home, but I longed to grow and make a greater impact in our community. I saw and heard there was a need and knew I could be the person to fulfill it, so I began the process of opening a small childcare center in our little town.

Over time my business grew, I opened a second center, and eventually combined the two to make one large childcare center. I loved every minute of it—the hard work, the research, the investment of time, and especially the day-to-day operations of interacting with the children and their families. But not everything is meant to last forever. The center started costing more to operate—as many expanding businesses do. Expenses and taxes increased, but as the bills and invoices stacked up, the income did not grow to match the costs. I detested the idea of continually increasing the rates as the cost of childcare can be a heavy burden to many families. Eventually, after running in the red for as long as we could, I made the difficult choice to let it go. I knew it was the right thing to do even though, for the very first time in years, I didn't have any idea what to do next. I was at a complete loss. I could live off the income from the sale of the center, but that wouldn't be sustainable long-term.

As time went on, I joked about enjoying "early retirement" when meeting friends for lunch or for an afternoon of coffee and crafts. I knew these relaxing days would come to an end but had no idea what that would look like or when it would happen. I didn't know what I wanted to do, didn't feel a calling or led in any direction, and no opportunities were presenting themselves. No doors seemed to be opening. I felt lost, and my confidence began to dwindle.

So, what do you do when you feel lost and without direction, when you have a restless, internal stirring you cannot shake, and you search for answers only to keep coming up empty? This is what I like to call "the waiting period." It's an in-between time or place in our lives, a temporary placeholder. One chapter has come to an end, the next chapter has yet to begin, and we have no idea what's going to be written. Waiting requires patience, but that doesn't mean we have to be passive. One day at a time, you wake up each morning and you keep going. Do what you can with each day, intentionally making the most of it. Strive to be the best version of yourself by helping others where you can, doing what you can, and talking to those whose paths cross yours. Stay positive, remain confident, and remind yourself this is just one of life's seasons, and seasons pass, so this time of waiting will also pass. Things have a way of working themselves out until our path becomes clear. During this time of unassured wandering, there are lessons to be learned here as well. Focus intently on your personal growth, take time to meditate and look inward, pray, journal, or go for walks in nature. Maintaining your forward direction is key, and what's meant for you will find its way to you in time, at the right time.

During my time of uncertainty, while brainstorming copious ideas and applying for jobs, I assisted in taking care of my then mother-in-law, who had dementia. Looking back, I treasure the moments spent with her. It was summer and pleasant enough weather that I was able to take her to do things she enjoyed while she could still enjoy them. We enjoyed trips to the pet store to look at the kittens and went out for ice cream, lots of ice cream.

I also aided my husband with his business, and one day someone came in and began talking about a job at a company he knew was hiring. My ears instantly perked up, and I felt like this could be the job for me. I gave the customer my resume and a few weeks later was employed doing a job I loved. Throughout my time of wandering, I kept a forward movement. I did what I could to add meaning to my life, I talked to others whose paths crossed mine and eventually, my new purpose found its way to me.

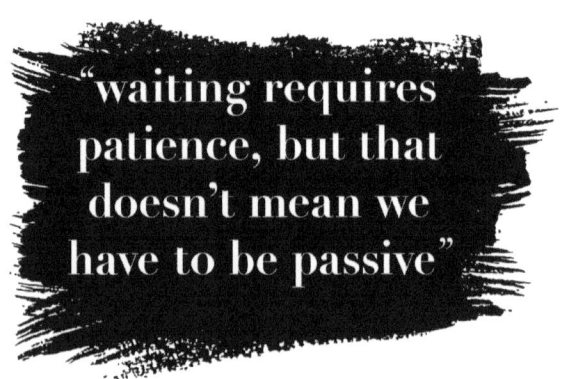

"waiting requires patience, but that doesn't mean we have to be passive"

you can't have it all at once

In the world we live in, it seems almost anything we could ever imagine is within reach. America: a beautiful place of abundance and "the land of opportunity." I believe that's why my dad worked so hard to ingrain into his kids the value of not living beyond your means, only purchasing what you can pay for, and keeping your nose out of the Joneses' business as they aren't worth keeping up with anyway. If your mind is focused on being grateful and satisfied with what you have—rather than focused on what you don't have—keeping up with anyone is the furthest worry from your mind.

The constant mixed messages we receive in our everyday lives are what make things confusing. We're encouraged to spend time and money on the things we want and desire. "Treat yourself," "You deserve that," "Buy the thing," "Book the trip," "YOLO (you only live once)!" Then two seconds later, we're encouraged to be content with what we have and where we are, learn how to declutter to live a more minimalist lifestyle, and save for retirement. I know my brain hurts and just like Veruca Salt, sometimes I want it all and I want it *now*.

While I believe you can have it all, you can do it all, and you can achieve it all, I also believe there is a time and a season for everything. A time to spend, and a time to save. A time to plan, and a time to chase. A time to prepare, and a time to act. You can have it all, you just typically can't (and this is the only time I'll use that word) have it all at once.

Before opening my first childcare center, I spent several years just thinking about the prospect of it: what it would look like, how it would work, various aspects of business ownership, and contemplated whether I should take the plunge. For years, I deliberated constantly, and the more I thought about opening a center, the clearer my ideas became—down to the smallest detail. When a dream or desire continues to flourish and grow, it's something you should pursue.

Moving to North Carolina was a dream I had for over *twenty years*! It was something I'd daydream about, unsure it would ever happen, but if it did, I'd most likely be retirement age. It was my someday dream that never went away. Desire grew, so when I was presented with an opportunity, I was determined not to let it pass me by.

Both were legitimate dreams, and I achieved them. However, they did not occur at the same time. There's no way I could have opened a business and moved to another state while raising a young family and going to school. Time and seasons, my friend; each has its precise place. The objective is that we do not stop thinking and dreaming. Those things tucked away in our hearts are achievable, and the hope of fulfilling them is one of the things that keep us moving forward.

busyness

Take a moment to self-reflect and ask yourself, "Is my over-commitment holding me back?" Oftentimes what keeps us from reaching our full potential is ourselves and the way we allow ourselves to become distracted by the necessary and/or unnecessary things that simultaneously pull us in several different directions, or simply keep us from focusing on the direction we are meant to be facing. Life presents us with many obligations and responsibilities daily, but how often do we allow ourselves to become distracted by tasks keeping us needlessly or unnecessarily busy?

Even as I write these words, I set a goal to be intentional, purposeful, and focused on exercising my passion—writing. Yet I check my phone multiple times waiting for news, and then become engrossed in something unnecessary. Weeks later when I reread what I've written, that unnecessary task is already forgotten. We are surrounded by things that keep us distracted and busy in today's world; things that give the impression of busyness, but at the end of the day are not at all productive.

There are a multitude of reasons we might keep ourselves busy. "I can't because I *have* to get this done today" can be a handy excuse to get out of an undesired obligation. We may keep busy to avoid having too much time alone with our thoughts and are trying to avoid what is going on inside our minds. Perhaps we stay busy because if we aren't hustling, we're afraid of being perceived as lazy in comparison to other people. I struggled with the notion of inferiority daily throughout my first marriage. Often, we choose to keep busy because the season of life we're in demands it.

These are just a few of the many reasons established, to keep us preoccupied or busy. Did any of these resonate with you? Take a moment to consider what keeps you unnecessarily preoccupied. I'm certain you can think of more things that hinder your priorities.

It's okay to slow down and place boundaries on the things that keep you busy. When my kids were in school and at the age when their friends started playing sports, they began showing interest in playing sports too. They had some friends who were involved in several activities at a time. I don't know how those families juggled evenings with multiple commitments. What I did know was I was our family's chauffeur who would take the kids to practices and games, make sure everyone had dinner and that the kitchen was clean before leaving, and then rush them to bed when we got home. I didn't need to know how those families had several kids in multiple sports or activities at the same time. I knew as a married "single" parent I would not be able to do what other families did, so I placed boundaries on our busyness. I told my kids they could play any sport or join any activity they wanted, but only one per child at a time. My son chose to play baseball and basketball, which worked out perfectly because when basketball ended, baseball season began. My daughter experimented with many different activities. She tried dance, gymnastics, field hockey, band, soccer, and a few other things, but never more than one at a time. I was able to balance our schedule and not feel overwhelmed or burnt out. I didn't worry over what everyone else's kids were doing, nor did I care what others' opinions were concerning our boundaries.

If you have little ones in public elementary school or belong to a church there may be an ongoing joke to not say "yes" when asked to volunteer, because once you commit to volunteer one time your name goes on the "yes" list. You will be the first person asked to help at every opportunity moving forward, with no regard to your time or other prior commitments. So many of us who enjoy helping struggle to say no in these instances. This leads to over-commitment and burnout. Consider this; your "yes" is someone else's "no". When we commit to doing something that does not fit into our lives, someone else out there may be blessed by that same opportunity. Rather than committing to "helping" out of a feeling of obligation, consider how the opportunity fits into your life at that moment in time. If it does not, give yourself grace for telling someone, "This isn't a good time for me but please keep me in mind for the next time." And know someone else will be presented with an opportunity that fits in their life at this moment in time.

You get to decide what's perfect for you. Maybe you need to limit your screen time, say no to someone who asks you to volunteer all the time, or start meal prepping on Sunday so you have more time throughout the week. Think about what keeps you busy and consider what boundaries you can put in place to help you intentionally set aside time for yourself and your goals.

procrastination

I'm not going to lie. If procrastination was a sport, I'd possess many gold medals. My biggest shortcoming is my ability to procrastinate. Without deadlines, most of the important things in my life would not get done in a timely manner. If I had it my way and no deadlines, there'd be an endless cycle of scrolling through social media reels, getting snacks, lying on the couch thinking about everything I should be doing, checking my phone again, and then deciding to go for a walk because it's a nice day. While I'm out, I may get inspired to be productive, but by the time I'm home again, I'll most likely start the cycle over. This only results in making myself feel guilty for putting things off I desperately want and need to accomplish.

When I do have a productive day and someone asks how my day was, I always say, over-excitedly, "It was great!" Productive days truly are great days, they just don't happen as often as I think they should, or I would like them to at times. I know how good it feels to be productive, and the internal joy of accomplishment, but it is far easier to put things off.

Why do we procrastinate? I know why I do. Just a second while I check my phone… Typically, I procrastinate because there are things I'd rather be doing other than what I *should* be doing. At times, laziness makes my desire to procrastinate stronger than my desire to get things done. As a perfectionist, I often tell myself, "There's no point in doing something unless it's going to be perfect," while knowing if it isn't going to be perfect, I'll have less interest in doing it. Procrastination is also a coping mechanism for stress when a task feels overwhelming, so I put those tasks off until the last possible minute.

There are a multitude of reasons why people procrastinate. If you tend to put things off like I do, look inward and determine *why* you procrastinate (assuming you don't already know) and create a plan for how to work through it. Then, you can move forward accordingly. Being a procrastinator doesn't have to hold you back from achieving your goals. It just may take a little longer to achieve them if you allow procrastination to take over.

 To get started, try creating your own deadlines, making a to-do list, breaking large jobs into smaller, more manageable tasks, completing the most difficult portion of your project first, and remember to reward yourself for a job well done.

One of my favorite tips is enlisting the help of an accountability partner. When you know someone is going to ask about your progress, you want to give them good news. No one wants to show up for a meeting with their accountability partner and report that no progress has been made. That trusted friend or loved one who checks in will also be your cheerleader, challenge you to keep going, encourage you to stay aligned with your goals, and push you forward even when the road gets rough.

Most importantly, give yourself grace—you've got this.

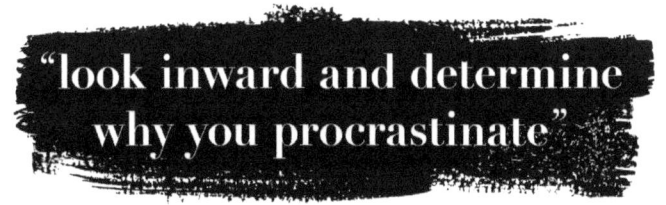

trust yourself

No one knows you better than you know yourself. Your innermost thoughts, fears, hopes, and dreams—sure, you may share some of these with those closest to you, those whom you trust. But it wouldn't surprise me if there are also things so uniquely you or so very personal that you choose to keep them hidden away, deep within your heart. These are the things that if we did choose to share them, others wouldn't understand the depth and the gravity of why we hold them so close to our heart.

Trust yourself to make the right decisions and do the right thing. You'll be able to feel if the timing is right, and you'll figure out if you're headed in the right direction, or if you need to take a step back, regroup, and change course. Eventually, your head and heart will agree about these realizations. Trust your gut! Generally, it doesn't steer you wrong, because we're built with intuition and instinct, we just tend to not listen for it; we're unable to hear it through all the noise, or we ignore our intuitive or instinctive feelings.

When I was in labor with my firstborn, I was five centimeters dilated. Twenty minutes later, I told the nurse, "I feel like I need to push." The doctor said, "There's no way you could completely dilate that quickly." Although it was almost twenty-five years ago, the most vivid memory of the evening as those moments unfolded was when the nurse told me, "No one knows your body better than you do." She had the doctor check me again, and sure enough, it was go time!

I have held tight to this over the years and since they have grown remind my children of this often, "No one knows your body better than you do."

The same is true in all aspects of our being. You know what's right for you and what's wrong for you. You know when you're about to do something you aren't supposed to, and how you'll feel if you do it anyway. You know when you're supposed to do something, and how it feels when you listen to the voice inside you and do it. You know when you're about to send a text you should probably delete, and how you'll feel if you send it anyway. You know when you should check in on someone you haven't talked to in a while, and you know how you feel when you ignore that inkling and don't reach out. It's that little voice within us that doesn't go away; it's there until you either listen to it or ignore it for so long that the moment is gone. I think you'll also find that if you ignore that voice for too long, the end of that road is where we find regret. That's why it's so important to listen to that inner voice—trust your gut, your intuition, that constant banter in your head that won't let something go—because it's pointing you in the direction you need to go.

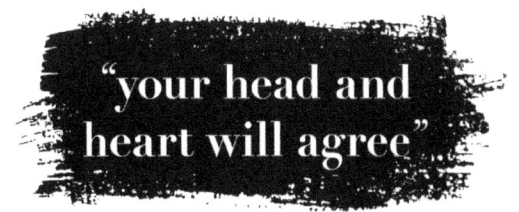

your destiny is inside you

Guilt washes over me when I feel like I'm talking someone into spending money they don't want to spend, or into buying something they don't want or need. Being a salesperson is not a talent I was given, so I've always shied away from those types of professions, and even farther away from multi-level marketing opportunities—it's just not where I shine. I'm not strong with math or Excel spreadsheets, and I have a terrible voice for singing. As self-aware as I am about my shortcomings, I also know where my strengths lie: child development, helping professions, organization, communication, listening, and encouragement. Those are also things I'm passionate about and feel confident putting effort into.

If I had gone into car sales or accounting, maybe I would've been able to financially survive, but I'm not sure I would have thrived. Going to work would feel like going to work. I certainly wouldn't be happy in the long run, and I may not have been successful because of that. I might've failed miserably due to a lack of interest in my career—thinking of myself as a failure. When really, the true reason I wouldn't be excelling in my profession would be because it's not where I was meant to be.

This is what I mean when I say your destiny is already inside you. Start with what you know to be true about yourself. Maybe you love cars, math or accounting, helping others, fashion, or organizing. Make a list of things you love and things you know you are passionate about and excel in. Make a second list of things you know are not your strengths or literally despise. Your destiny will not veer far from who you are as a person. Instead, it will embrace every part of who you are—not only what you love and what you're good at, but also what you care deeply about.

Consider making two lists right now, one of your strengths and the things you are passionate about and another list of things you know you would do absolutely anything to avoid. After making these lists, take some time to reflect and consider if any revealing thoughts emerged.

Strengths/Passions   **Dislikes**

1.

2.

3.

4.

5.

6.

7.

8.

mistakes

You're probably going to make mistakes along the way. Maybe that's not something you want or need to hear, but it shouldn't come as a surprise either. We all make mistakes and will continue to do so as imperfect, fallible beings. What may be a surprise is that *it's okay to make mistakes*. It's okay to forgive yourself, put it behind you, and move forward. We're all imperfect beings, so when you make a mistake, give yourself grace, forgive yourself, learn from it, and then move on. Treasure the lessons and leave the rest behind.

Many of us tend to be hard on ourselves after making a mistake, worrying that people are judging us, or that our mistakes will follow us, forever defining our character. Sometimes, we just plain give up because we dwell on the mistake and not the lesson; we allow mistakes to keep us from moving forward because we're afraid to repeat them.

If you do make a mistake (believe me, I've made many), own it. Acknowledge the fact that—oops—it wasn't the right thing to do. If others are involved, be honest and sincerely remorseful, make amends, and apologize. This includes apologizing to yourself, then give yourself grace and remind yourself that it's in the past now. You can't go back in time. It's over, it's behind you—leave it there. Move forward focusing on the lesson, learn from your mistakes, adjust, course correct, and keep moving forward. It sounds so simple, doesn't it? Yet we make it so complicated. We dwell on it and can't let go because our inner dialogue just won't shut up about it. We have difficulty course correcting because we fixate on what went wrong or how we could have done things better or differently. Give yourself the grace to allow it to be *that simple*.

Even for mistakes that feel as if they carry a heavier weight, the same rules apply. It may take longer to put those heavy burdens in your rearview mirror, but give yourself grace daily until the job is done—it's the only way forward. Don't worry about the people whom you *think* are judging you—they might be or they may not be, but one thing's for sure: everyone else is out there making mistakes too.

change is not optional

Change is one thing you can always count on. It's not optional. We will always be guaranteed change occurring in the world, in our circumstances, and within ourselves as we grow. Sometimes, change is predictable, and other times completely unpredictable, but we must embrace the fact that change is inevitable. If you're someone who doesn't really care for change, I encourage you to learn to embrace it. No, it's not always easy. Even good changes can present challenges and be difficult. It forces us to step outside our comfort zone, leave behind the familiar, disrupt our routine, and present us with new challenges. But we're transformed through change; it promotes healthy inner growth, encouraging us to revamp our perspective with the thrill of new experiences.

Perhaps you are someone who embraces change. If so, you're in good company, as I, personally, love and crave change. I rearrange furniture often, try new restaurants, go to various grocery stores, listen to a wide array of music, and it's why I moved to the beach—because I view change as an adventure! I get to see something new, try something different, meet new people, do something I've never done before, learn about the world around me, and learn more about myself in the process. If I don't like whatever is changing in my life, I know that's okay too, because nothing is permanent—I can always revert, move on to something else, or just wait it out. Because of change, we're never stuck indefinitely—we have options, and our circumstances are not locked in.

If embracing change is a challenge, try embracing a growth mindset. See yourself as capable and open to challenge and change. Remind yourself, "I'm excited to take on this new adventure and all that lies before me." Intentionally focus on the possibilities before you rather than what is left behind and remember, it's temporary; at some point, your new will become your new normal.

Let's try an exercise together. Look back on your life and make a list of five changes that have occurred. I want to see if most of those changes either ended up being positive or if you were able to take something positive from those experiences. These changes could be a major event like getting married, having children, or moving to a new city, or something as simple as making a new friend, starting to go to the gym, or adding a pet to your family. Once you've made your list, recall how you felt about each change when it happened. How do you feel about it now? Then ask yourself, "Did I learn anything about myself from this event? If so, what did I learn about myself through that experience?"

Five Changes That Have Occurred:

1.

2.

3.

4.

5.

Throughout each change that has happened and all the changes yet to come, celebrate your growth.

let's not compare

I've often heard people say, "I'm not going to complain about my problems, because other people have it much worse." Perhaps you've said this phrase yourself at one time or another, or at least thought the same thing. It is true, that not everyone has the same challenges to overcome, and some experience very difficult things. However, what one person is going through does not diminish what you are going through, the struggles you face, the feelings attached to that struggle, or the impact on your life, health, and well-being.

If you often compare your struggles to someone else's, it's time to refocus. We shouldn't compare ourselves to anyone else and should instead have empathy and compassion for both them and us. If we see, hear of, or know someone struggling through a difficult time, offer them help and be supportive without comparing our troubles to theirs, or their troubles to someone else's.

Minimizing or avoiding our feelings and emotions attached to our circumstances because we are comparing ourselves to others will hinder us from pursuing the self-care and healing we need to move forward.

Each situation we face has the potential to strengthen our character and be used for growth.

unlearning what life is "supposed to look like"

Do you have a specific idea of what you feel life is "supposed to look like" or how it's supposed to unfold? If so, where did that idea come from? Take some time to really think about who or what it was that molded your perspective of idealistic adulthood—whether it was your parents, other family members, TV, church, or the lack of one or more of these in your life. None of these is inherently bad or good but remember: change is the only constant. Times have changed, people have changed, and our world has changed.

I stayed in a toxic marriage for years because that's what was expected. I grew up saying I'd never get divorced, because the values instilled in me opposed the concept of divorce; my husband knew that and used it to his advantage.

By no means am I telling anyone to get a divorce, make a life-altering decision, or question any decision that is based on your values, but I am encouraging a constant reevaluation. In all situations, be empowered to think freely and independently, and make decisions based on your understanding—without judgment—and with full support.

Life is not a precise mold that forms humans in the same pattern—it looks different for everyone, and it's supposed to. It's OK to permit ourselves to undo what we think "living our best life" *should* look like based on the influence of others. In this world, we're offered diversity, and we need to encourage one another as we move along our individual, various paths. Diversity is the one commonality among all human beings, and the beautiful relationships we form are what makes life worth living. Let's use our differences to build stronger bridges, learn from each other, and support and empower each other. There are people doing amazing things in totally unconventional ways, and not only surviving but thriving. You, too, can do whatever sets your life apart—the expectation to fit into a cookie-cutter mold no longer exists.

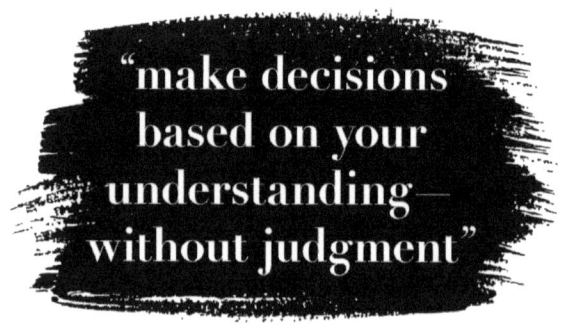

"make decisions based on your understanding—without judgment"

self-determination

Before the discovery of my second husband's affair, I began the year excited to watch his swearing-in ceremony as he was recently elected mayor of our small town. This was a goal we'd spent the entire previous year campaigning for. He'd worked hard to reach this moment in his life, and I fully supported him every step of the way. Finally, his shining moment was before us, and I was happy to be "the woman behind the man," his ambitious supporter who had helped him achieve this extraordinary goal of his. I was proud to be his biggest supporter, his avid helper, and his champion.

Little did I know that not even three-hundred-sixty-five days later I'd close out my year five hundred miles away sitting on a wooden bench in a sleepy little beach town, listening to the sound of the waves crashing in front of me and the music of "The Cascades" playing in the background. It was late December, and the beach was all but empty. Just a few locals taking an afternoon walk and someone in the background cleaning out their car while *Rhythm of the Rain* soothed our souls. How quickly, how unexpectedly, and how drastically things can change sometimes. Sitting beside the ocean, taking in my surroundings and the peacefulness of it all, I reflected on the previous year and peace came over me. I knew everything that happened—every bad thing, every tear, every heartache, all the confusion, and all the decisions I had to make—led me to this moment where I felt absolute peace. I knew I was exactly where I was meant to be. Whatever lay before me was also undoubtedly meant for me, and I was no longer afraid.

There were some decisions I had no say in, things thrown my way I'd rather not have faced, and many challenges to overcome. I was knocked down harder than ever, but after taking it day by day for a while, I picked up the pieces and put myself back together. I had many decisions to make—most importantly refusing to allow my situation to determine my outcome. I was determined to turn the negative into a positive, so I changed my thinking from believing something was taken away from me, to believing I was given an opportunity. I was down *bigtime*—hell, I was down for a while, but I chose not to stay there. It wasn't where I belong, and it's not where you belong either. You have the power to put the pieces together and refuse to allow any person or situation to rob you from the blessed life you desire and deserve. Gradually you'll turn any negatives into positives!

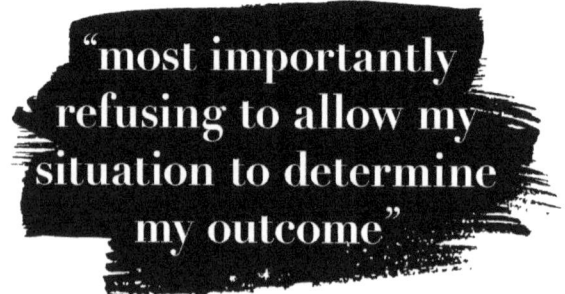

embrace yourself and what you believe

Your destiny is who you are and has been inside you from the beginning—all that's left is for you to take the first step. I don't know how many people take that scary, uncomfortable, unfamiliar step toward an unknown future. You will undergo many inevitable changes, but if you walk confidently in the direction of your dreams, what's meant for you will find you.

As you embark on this crusade of self-discovery—pursuing passions ablaze with possibility—believe in yourself and your ability to achieve what you set out to do. Believe in your strength, wisdom, power, understanding, resilience, and constant growth. Imagine the path illuminating before you and opportunities presenting themselves. But if they do not, realize it's only for your benefit—those closed doors are not currently meant for you, or you're being protected from a wrong turn. Effectively communicate your needs along the way and accept support from those closest to you. Utilize the necessary resources to be successful in your endeavors and believe in the outcome you envision for your life. Trust that your hard work and sacrifice will be worth it in the end and will manifest a brighter future.

Every single one of us is put on this planet for a specific purpose. All your likes, dislikes, interests, gifts, talents, and experiences mold you and point you in the direction of your purpose. These things prepare you, transform you—showing who you are and the path you're meant to take. All the negative encounters and good experiences will formulate together to shape your best life—if you allow them.

No matter where you are, how old you are, what you want to hide, wish you could change, have gone through, are going through or will go through—it will all come together. Be proud of your journey, embrace each piece, and believe in yourself more because of it. *You were born for this.*

"believe in yourself and your ability to achieve what you set out to do"

rebel queen

We hope you loved Robyn's book as much as we loved partnering with her to prepare it for you! She is an amazing inspiration for all women to find strength and hope.

With a combined 20+ years in publishing, we know how to help anyone write, launch, and market a book. So if a book is on your bucket list? We're the team to take it from brain dump to bestseller.

RebelQueen.co
marti@rebelqueen.co
Facebook and Instagram @rebelqueenbooks

Now that you've finished reading The Desire to Love Myself, write a review on the Amazon or Goodreads listing to help other readers find the book that is best for them.

Robyn is available for coaching or speaking engagements for small or large groups and workshops.

Visit **robynmichelle.life** for details.

www.ingramcontent.com/pod-product-compliance
Lightning Source LLC
Chambersburg PA
CBHW052131030426
42337CB00028B/5111